LET THE CHALL

It's kind of an odd grouping, isn't it—*desert* snakes? I mean, it bears no taxanomic parallel; there's no family or genus that encompasses the "desert" snakes. So where's the common thread here?

In natural history terms, we tie these snakes together in regards to habitat, which means, on the keeping level, they are joined in regards to housing. The snakes of and milk snakes. They may say they 'only keep kings and milks,' but there are others in that group that certainly aren't tri-colored in any way. And some people only keep land turtles, i.e., box turtles and tortoises. These turtles are not of the same genera or even the same family, but again, the lines are drawn based on housing considerations.

For the most part, desert

Desert-dwelling snakes pose a true challenge to even the most experienced herpetoculturists. Information on the captive care of many species, however, is scant at best and therefore desperately needed. This beautiful Colorado Desert Shovelnose Snake, *Chionactis occipitalis annulata*, for example, is easy to maintain and yet is rarely kept and has never been bred.

the North American deserts all live in roughly the same type of ecological niche, and within that niche is a whole little world all its own.

Hobbyists often govern the type of herptiles they keep by strange parameters. For example, some folks only keep tri-colored king snakes are largely ignored by hobbyists. Why? Well, I can't say for sure. The main factor probably is lack of availability. When was the last time you saw a shovelnose snake, *Chionactis* sp., or a leafnose snake, *Phyllorhynchus* sp., in a pet shop? The logic is very simple—you can't buy what you can't find.

But desert snakes can be very *challenging,* and that's where their true appeal lies. In *any* hobby there are ascending levels of ability. Some desert snakes can be tougher than others, and those I do not recommend for beginners. However, there are others, and we'll discuss them in this book, that even the most inexperienced keeper will be able to maintain (and maybe even breed!).

The point is, the aim of this book is to guide you towards the thrill of a true challenge by "turning you on" to a generally overlooked but nevertheless fascinating group of snakes that most definitely is worth considering as terrarium subjects. I'll go into which North American desert snakes are easy to keep and which aren't, and then perhaps you'll want to approach them with an aim towards upward mobility, i.e., as your keeping skills improve and your confidence grows, you'll want to try keeping snakes of progressive difficulty.

Here's an incentive—some of the tougher ones have yet to be bred in captivity, so maybe you'll end up breaking new ground. If you do, please don't keep it a secret; such information is quite valuable to the rest of the herpetocultural community. TFH now has a herpetological/ herpetocultural magazine called *Reptile Hobbyist,* so if you have any really interesting husbandry or breeding information, let the editors know.

All in all, my goal with this book is to suggest something a little different, something kind of new. 'New' often is looked upon as a good thing, and I have found that most people keep an open mind towards new things. Keeping snakes of the North American deserts can at times be both painful and pleasurable, but *never* is it dull.

So let the challenge begin...

W. P. Mara

Some desert-dwelling snakes are, of course, more difficult to keep than others. This Western Leafnose Snake, *Phyllorhynchus decurtatus perkinsi,* for example, is considered one of the toughest of all North American desert snakes to maintain. More than 90% of all specimens die within the first few months of captivity.

PHOTO BY W. P. MARA.

PHOTO BY W. P. MARA.

Dr. Roger Conant signing autographs at the Mid-Atlantic Reptile Show in Baltimore, Maryland, September of 1993.

DEDICATION

When I think of the deserts of North America in conjunction with great herpetologists, one name often comes to mind—Dr. Roger Conant. I won't attempt to summarize all of his astonishing accomplishments in this tiny dedication paragraph. I will only say that he deserves the gratitude of contemporary herpetoculturists everywhere for all he has done to fortify the collective knowledge of the hobby we all now enjoy.

THE SNAKES IN QUESTION

As I already have said and undoubtedly will say again, some desert-dwelling North American snakes are fairly easy to maintain in captivity, while others most definitely are not. This is exactly how I've decided to arrange them here. I've outlined the housing, feeding, and breeding requirements of each snake group gleaned through recorded captive history (such as the domestic breeding of the Banded Sand Snake, which has yet to be accomplished), was built from whatever natural history records I could find. Also remember that any snake born in captivity from a female that was already gravid at the time of capture is not, in the

PHOTO BY ZOLTAN TAKACS.

A 'desert' is characterized by dry, sandy (basically infertile) soil and little or no vegetation. Shown is Joshua Tree National Park in California.

(which in itself is set up by genus), then classified them by way of a three-level system—1/ Easy, 2/Moderate, and 3/ Difficult. My opinions as to which groups should go where are based on the personal experiences of both myself and others. Any information that could not be general opinion of most herpetoculturists, a captive-bred animal.

The keeping of venomous snakes is geared only for experienced professionals, most of whom already know plenty about the difficulties involved in keeping and breeding the more

If you happen to live in an area where desert snakes occur, it is logical to furnish the enclosure you keep your specimens in with materials found locally. The idea, overall, is to create an 'accurate' desert biotope.

challenging snake species. Snakes that are potentially deadly should not be kept by anyone except those who need them for professional purposes (in labs, zoos, etc.).

Finally, I should clarify what I mean by a North American 'desert' snake. The definition isn't as simple as 'a snake that lives in the western half of the United States,' as some may think. The central factor, again, is the habitat. If the group (genera) in question contains snakes that live in a definable desert habitat, then it is a desert group. Of course, some groups will have more desert snakes than others, i.e.,

the king and Milk snakes, genus *Lampropeltis*, are made up largely of non-desert species, whereas virtually all of the shovelnose snakes, genus *Chionactis*, are desert-dwellers.

LEVEL 1—The Easy Stuff

KING AND MILK SNAKES
Genus *LAMPROPELTIS*
Fitzinger, 1843

The kingsnakes and the Milk Snake, which undoubtedly are among the most popular snakes in the world, usually don't grow over a length of 60 in/152.4 cm and therefore are ideally suited for 20- or 30-gallon glass aquariums.

Adult pairs obviously will do better in the latter. Smaller specimens can be placed in 10s. It should be pointed out that most kings and Milks live in habitats other than desert, so make a point of finding out where your particular specimen(s) came from. Desert-dwelling specimens will require a substrate of sand with some gravel mixed in. A few rocks are necessary, as is a hidebox and household bulb, with a photoperiod of around 12 hours per day.

Feeding kings and Milks is a fairly painless affair. Most are ravenous rodent-eaters. Due to their relatively small size, they shouldn't be given anything larger than adult mice (large rats are positively out of the question). It should be mentioned that many neonatal *Lampropeltis* stubbornly

PHOTO BY W. P. MARA.

The Gray-banded Kingsnake, *Lampropeltis alterna*, is one of the most popular desert species, kept and bred by thousands of herpetoculturists worldwide. It is a beautiful and mild-tempered animal that also is fairly easy to breed. Sadly, however, the mortality rate among newborns is fairly high.

a climbing branch or two. The waterbowl should be sturdy since kings and Milks can easily tip those that are light weight. Heating is best provided via an undertank heating pad, and the "high" zone should be around 86°F/30°C. Lighting can be provided by way of an ordinary refuse all foods except small lizards and snakes, so that's one problem you may find yourself dealing with. However, many can be weaned onto easier-to-supply items either by scenting or through the use of a pinkie pump. Same goes for any of the adults.

Breeding for this genus is pretty much standard as with any other egglaying North American colubrid, so refer to the breeding chapter for information. Average incubation time for kings and Milks is around 75 to 90 days, and the average clutch size is between three and 12 eggs. Keep the newborns in separate enclosures since instances of cannibalism are not uncommon.

kept in a 20-gallon aquarium, either singularly or in pairs. Usable substrates can vary from sand, gravel, and wood chips to paper towels and indoor/outdoor carpeting. If you use either of the latter substrates, you should provide the animal(s) with a hidebox. If you any of the former, make the layer deep enough so the snake can burrow. A profusion of rocks will provide

PHOTO BY W. P. MARA.

Unlike many other desert-dwelling snakes, most king and Milk Snakes, genus *Lampropeltis*, are readily obtainable in pet shops. Most do well in captivity and can be tamed. Photo of a Honduran Milk Snake, *Lampropeltis triangulum hondurensis*.

ROSY BOAS
Genus *LICHANURA*
Cope, 1861

The beautiful Rosy Boa (there only is one species) has become tremendously popular in recent years and does remarkably well in captivity. Since it does not often grow over 36 in/91 cm, it can be

further shelter. Some sturdy branches will add a touch of naturalism to the setup, but the snake probably won't climb on them. A small sturdy waterbowl is required, but if the enclosure doesn't have good ventilation, only put the bowl in for a little while each day. Heat can be provided

PHOTO BY ZOLTAN TAKACS.

Because the deserts of North America are fairly hot during the day, many of the snakes that live there only come out during evening and night hours. Thus, a keeper must understand that his or her snakes may be visible only during these times. Above, Death Valley National Monument in southern California. Below, the Queretaro Kingsnake, *Lampropeltis ruthveni*, a popular nocturnal species.

PHOTO BY ISABELLE FRANCAIS.

through either an undertank heating pad or a spot lamp. Temperature gradient for this animal should be between 77 and 95°F/25 to 35°C during the day, with a five-degree drop during the night. Lighting can be ordinary Tungsten, with a photoperiod of about ten hours per day.

Most Rosy Boas are willing and eager feeders, which is one reason they're such good captives. Every now and then you'll get a specimen that needs to be force-fed, but this stubbornness rarely lasts long. Some only eat under the cover of darkness, so if your own specimen refuses food during the day, try offering food at night. Small mice, both live and pre-

Mos of s wan a sm herp item

Rosy Boas, *Lichanura trivirgata*, are attractive and m without fuss. They have become a cult favorite among h bred in captivity. Shown is courtship behavior betw *trivirgata*.

PHOTO BY ISABELLE FRANCAIS.

Most *Lampropeltis* can be sustained on a diet of small rodents. This Gray-banded King, *L. alterna*, for example, seems to be interested in this baby rat. Be aware, however, that many newborn specimens stubbornly refuse rodents and instead will take only small reptiles.

Since a desert is such a specific and sharply character[...] that its tenant animals have become specially adapted[...] impossible for most of them to survive elsewhere. *Crotalus scutulatus*, seen in the foreground, for examp[...] like a swamp or a rainforest.

PHOTO BY K. H. SWITAK.

When they feel threatened, Rosy Boas often will wrap themselves in a tight ball and hide their heads. From this, you can pretty much figure out that they are passive creatures that only lash out when they feel there is no other effective mode of defense at their disposal.

killed, should be taken. Other items include lizards, small snakes (including venomous species), and small birds.

The Rosy Boa is now being bred more than ever before. Why it has suddenly become so popular is a mystery. It can be hibernated in its normal quarters and at surprisingly low temperatures—as low as 40°F/4°C. Of course, a more reasonable number is around 52°F/11°C. Duration of hibernation should be around three months. From there, breeding is pretty much standard if you follow the steps outlined in the breeding chapter. The Rosy Boa is viviparous, meaning it gives birth to living young rather than laying eggs. After a gestation period of between 103 and 134 days, it will have a litter of between one and 12 (usually four or five) foot-long (or thereabouts) snakes.

BULL, PINE, AND GOPHER SNAKES
Genus *PITUOPHIS*
Holbrook, 1842

Being fairly large (six-foot specimens are not at all unusual) and husky (adults having the width of a baseball at midbody are not uncommon), the snakes of the genus *Pituophis* will need a good-sized enclosure—anything less than a 55-gallon for an adult pair would be cruel. A substrate of 100 % sand or 75 % sand with a 25 % soil content will do fine. A group of rocks also will be appreciated, as will some sturdy climbing branches. Live plants will end up getting crushed. A *sturdy* waterbowl is necessary, but it need not be overly large. Daytime temperatures of around 84°F/ 29°C will be fine, with a nighttime drop to around 74°F/23°C. Heating is best offered via an undertank heating pad or a spot

person who has ever successfully kept a shovelnose) offer the latter almost exclusively. If I come across a spider or a centipede, I'll throw it into the enclosure, but for the most part, crickets are the staple.

Notably, and this is something that came as a shock to many, my enclosure. The next morning, all the crickets were gone. A few weeks later, after offering a few more crickets, I crept into the room in the middle of the night with a flashlight, and lo and behold, I actually witnessed my big female with two spindly cricket legs sticking out her

PHOTO BY K. H. SWITAK.

Since the shovelnoses are so easy to keep in captivity, why haven't they been bred? Probably because no one has ever tried. This is the reason *many* snakes have never been captive-bred. All keepers should make an effort to propagate at least one 'untried' species. Photo of Mojave Shovelnose Snake, *Chionactis occipitalis occipitalis.*

shovelnoses eat only *dead* crickets. Not just dead, but *frozen-and-thawed* (and dusted with multivitamin powder). When I first got my specimens, I offered them live crickets, and they certainly seemed to want them, but they couldn't catch them. So, on a whim, I placed a handful of crickets in a sandwich bag and stuck them in my freezer. The next day, I thawed them (by laying them on an undertank heating pad, which did the job in under ten minutes), and placed them on a flat rock in the snakes'

mouth. Unbelievable!

In any case, my point is, if you decide to take a shot at keeping shovelnoses, this is the feeding approach I suggest you take. And remember—you should only offer food during the night. if you offer it during the day, it'll rot by the time they come up for it.

As far as I know, captive-breeding has not be achieved with any of the shovelnoses (if anyone has done it, please write to TFH and let us know!). However, this simply may be a case of 'no one's ever done it before.' It can be assumed a short cooling period is required, probably for two months at about 55°F/13°C. Shovelnoses are egglayers, and their clutches are quite small—more than four eggs in one clutch would be outstanding. Newborn specimens that came from wild-caught females have pretty much resembled their parents in every way. They are, as one might imagine, remarkably tiny. Thankfully, however, they seem to be very willing feeders, taking pinhead crickets and other tiny bugs without fuss.

GLOSSY SNAKES

Genus *ARIZONA*
Kennicott, 1859
Although very closely related to the Pine, Bull, and Gopher snakes, genus *Pituophis*, the glossy snakes are a bit smaller and therefore easier to manage in captivity, particularly in regards to housing. The largest specimens will grow only to about 70 in/178 cm, but the average is more like 55 in/139.7 cm. Thus, a pair of adults can be kept in a 20- or 30-gallon aquarium without too much of a problem. A reasonable substrate would be sand, soil, or a combination of both. Gravel also works well. Cage decor should include some type of secure hiding area, a few sturdy branches for climbing, and a sturdy waterbowl. Heat can be provided either by an undertank heating pad or a spot lamp, and the temperature should be around 83°F/28°C during the day, with a five degree drop during the night. Make sure the ventilation is good because the enclosure needs to stay fairly dry.

As far as feeding is concerned, the glossy snakes are mouse- and lizard-eaters. Most specimens will take either with equal relish, but every now and then you may end up with a stubborn lizard-only dieter. In such a case, reported captive histories tell us you can wean these snakes onto mice by "scenting" a pre-killed mouse—rubbing it against the body of a lizard. If you end up having to do

this, I advise you keep a small setup with some common lizards, these being your "scenters." The entire weaning process, from the day of the first "scented meal" until the snake begins to willingly accept unscented mice, can take anywhere from six weeks to four

Glossy snakes, genus *Arizona*, are handsome, hardy, and even-tempered. They are very closely related to the snakes of the genus *Pituophis*. Photo of an Kansas Glossy Snake, *Arizona elegans elegans*, by K. H. Switak.

months, and then there are the few specimens that simply will not allow themselves to be weaned, ever.

Breeding glossy snakes has been achieved many times in captivity. Like the snakes of the genus *Pituophis*, glossys are very willing breeders. The young are very pretty, resembling the parents almost exactly, and most will take newborn mice from the start. Glossy snakes breed in the spring after a two- to three-month

period of hibernation at a temperature of about 52°F/11°C. Gestation lasts about 80 days, after which time the female lays a clutch of anywhere from three to 23 eggs (which are almost two and a half inches long). These eggs take up to three months to hatch, which is close to "standard" for a North American colubrid.

LYRE SNAKES

Genus *TRIMORPHODON*
Cope, 1861

These attractive rear-fanged vipers have been overlooked by the herpetocultural community for far too long. They are moderate in size, nicely patterned (some experts think they may be rattlesnake mimics, which will give you some idea as to their appearance), and fairly intelligent, which means they can be tamed with time and patience.

An adult pair of lyres can be kept in a 30-gallon enclosure. A 20-gallon would be fine for a single adult specimen (although you'll certainly want to take a shot at breeding these fascinating serpents). The ideal substrate is sand, but soil or finely crushed walnut shells will do in a pinch. Gravel also is acceptable. Cage decor must include some relatively large stones, preferably

Glossy snakes have been bred by a few dedicated culturists and apparently are very willing subjects. The young look very much like the adults and, as is the case with most snakes, adapt to captivity much better than wild-caught specimens. Photo of a Desert Glossy Snake, *Arizona elegans eburnata*.

PHOTO BY K. H. SWITAK.

The only problem a keeper may encounter with glossy snakes is the desire of some specimens to eat only lizards. In such a case, it is advised that you 'scent' dead mice by rubbing them on a lizard's body and then slowly wean your stubborn glossy(s) onto rodents over the course of a few months. Above, a Texas Glossy Snake, *Arizona elegans eburnata*. Below, an Arizona Glossy Snake, *Arizona elegans noctivaga*.

PHOTO BY R. D. BARTLETT.

flat ones, because lyre snakes like to wedge themselves into the cracks and crevaces of rock walls in the wild. Thus, as long as you provide such spaces, a hidebox will not be necessary. In either case, some type of hiding area must be offered because lyres are strictly nocturnal and will become highly stressed if they are left exposed during light hours. Branches and desert plants will add a nice visual touch, and the snakes may in fact spend some time climbing on the former. A small waterbowl also is necessary. Heating should be provided via a large undertank heating pad, although "room heat" also works well. Ideal temperature is around 85°F/30°C during the day, with a drop of about eight degrees during the night. The enclosure should be kept quite dry and exposed to a photoperiod of about ten hours of light per day.

Getting a lyre snake to eat rarely is a problem. Every specimen that I have ever kept (and, for that matter, every specimen kept by friends of mine), has accepted mice or small rats without any fuss whatsoever. It should be pointed out that wild specimens also feverishly hunt and consume lizards, so if you have the opportunity to offer a few, do so. Most specimens will accept frozen-and-thawed rodents right from the start, which is a great convenience. Be careful of overfeeding, because these snakes love to eat once they get going.

As I implied before, breeding lyre snakes is not all that difficult; I know of many keepers who have

done so. In fact, if you have the chance, try to track down two very good articles on the subject—"Reproductive Behavior in the California Lyre Snake, *Trimorphodon biscutatus vandenburghi*" by Thomas M. Mills (in the Southwestern

The lyre snakes, genus *Trimorphodon*, undoubtedly are among the most underrated North American serpents. They are strikingly patterned and colored, moderate in size, easy to house, and willing rodent feeders. There even have been a number of carefully recorded captive-breedings. Photo of a Sonoran Lyre Snake, *Trimorphodon biscutatus lambda*, by Ken Lucas.

Herpetologist's Society newsletter, *HERPETOLOGY*, Vol. 23, No. 1, April, 1993), and "The Captive Care of the California Lyre Snake, *Trimorphodon biscutatus vandenburghi*" by David J. Zoffer (*Reptile Hobbyist*, Vol. 1, No. 3, January/February, 1996).

Encouraging a mating response in these snakes seems to involve the joining of not two but three specimens, these being a female and two males. The two males should go through some sort of ritualistic combat, and you should be able to discern the dominant specimen fairly quickly. After removing the "loser," the the remaining two snakes should mate without problem. Gestation apparently is relatively short—between 30 and 50 days. Egg clutch size varies from between six to a dozen. Incubation lasts about 70 days, and the hatchlings look very much like their parents. Reports say they accept unscented pinkie mice without

any problem whatsoever, which is wonderful mews for any keeper. They are lively and alert, biting without hesitation, but again, with time and patience they can be tamed.

One final note—the reason lyre snakes have been included in the "moderately challenging" section rather than under the "easy stuff" heading is because they are rear-fanged, which may turn off some keepers. In the interests of safety, I am not going to say these snakes are totally harmless to man, but I will point out that it is generally accepted in the herpetological community that their venom is believed to be ineffective against humans, and

The worry most prospective keepers of lyre snakes have is that these snakes are rear-fanged and thus mildly venomous. However, no human fatalities have ever been recorded as a result of a lyre snake bite. Photo of a Texas Lyre Snake, *Trimorphodon biscutatus vilkinsoni.*

PHOTO BY K. H. SWITAK.

PHOTO BY W. P. MARA.

Longnose Snakes, *Rhinocheilus lecontei*, have been part of the commercial pet trade for years in spite of the fact that most are very difficult to maintain in captivity. The main problem lies in their feeding habits—they are devout lizard-eaters. Shown is a *Rhinocheilus lecontei "clarus."*

that no deaths ever have been reported in connection with their bite. I, in fact, have been bitten twice by an adult female, and in neither instance did I suffer any adverse effects whatsoever.

LEVEL 3—The Tough Stuff

LONGNOSE SNAKES
  Genus *RHINOCHEILUS*
  Baird and Girard, 1853
  Longnose snakes have long been a pet-shop staple in spite of the difficulties involved in keeping them. They are relatively small and demure, and are quite pretty.
  Being small (rarely over 41 in/ 104 cm), an adult pair can be kept in a 20- or 30-gallon aquarium. Substrates can vary from the naturalistic sand or soil to the store-bought gravel, finely crushed walnut shells, artifical turf, or paper toweling. Since longnoses like to burrow and remain hidden for most of the day, I would advise the two naturalistic beddings. Cage decor must include a few good-sized stones, a small waterbowl, and maybe a branch or two. If you are not going to provide them with a deep layer of substrate, then a tight and dark hidebox must also be included. Daytime temperatures should be around 82°F/28°C with only a small drop at night since these snakes are almost wholly nocturnal and therefore will need some nighttime heat. An undertank heating pad

One attribute Longnose Snakes certainly have is an almost austere beauty, as you can see in these two Texas Longnoses, *Rhinocheilus lecontei tessellatus*. (Notice also the slight variation in color and pattern between the two specimens.) Another nice thing about them is their docility; most specimens never bite. Photo by K. H. Switak.

works well for the daytime heat, but a ceramic heat emitter is the ideal tool for providing night warmth. The enclosure should be kept free of moisture and should be submitted to a photoperiod of no more than ten hours per day. Since these snakes are particularly susceptible to stress, you may want to consider partially covering their enclosure during daylight hours.

Feeding is the hard part with longnose snakes. Most are stubbornly devout lizard-munchers. Even the ever-popular "weaning" technique rarely works with these aggravating little beasts. Let me say that some specimens will eat mice or small rats without too much fuss (the Mexican Longnose Snake, *Rhinocheilus antoni,* for example, is a reliable mouser), but the majority (probably around 80 %) will not. Of course, there always is the option of force-feeding pre-killed mice until the snake

develops a liking for them, but in recent years I have come to feel that force-feeding is not really even a viable option anymore, except in extreme or unusual cases. A snake that is being constantly force-fed will become stressed and may die. Even if it doesn't, it won't have much of a captive life, and then what's the point of keeping it at all? Do you really want a snake you have to force-feed all the time? Doesn't sound like a very enjoyable hobby to me. So, unless you can get lizards on a regular basis, or you get lucky enough to obtain a longnose that takes mice right from the start (which, again, is a rarity), you shouldn't even consider keeping these snakes in the first place.

Breeding, surprisingly, has been achieved with some longnoses. Dr. John V. Rossi, veterinarian and herpetoculturist extraordinaire from northern Florida, has done it, as have

Longnose Snakes seem particularly susceptible to stress in captivity. They are nocturnal creatures that like to roam, so it comes as no surprise that the inherent restrictions of a captive environment greatly upset them. Photo of a Texas Longnose, *Rhinocheilus lecontei tessellatus.*

PHOTO BY W. P. MARA.

others. I have been given gravid specimens and hatched their eggs, but I have never actually mated an adult pair.

Apparently, once you "get them going" in captivity, it seems they will mate without too much trouble. They are spring breeders, have a gestation period of about two months, and lay a small (four to nine) clutch of white, elongate

HOOKNOSE SNAKES

Genera *FICIMIA* and *GYALOPION*

Gray, 1849 and Cope, 1861 respectively

Hooknose snakes are tiny creatures, none growing more than 19 in/48 cm. Because of this, they can be kept quite comfortably in 10- or 20-gallon aquariums. Since they are true

PHOTO BY K. H. SWITAK.

Although beautiful, the hooknose snakes also are very secretive. In a way, this makes them poor captives because their keepers will never see them! Photo of a Western Hooknose Snake, *Gyalopion canum.*

eggs, which can be incubated in the "standard" manner. The young, which measure up to 10 in/25 cm, are, believe it or not, considerably less attractive than the adults, with large black saddles and spotty, almost nondescript underpatterning. Like the adults, they are particularly difficult to get feeding. They like very small lizards and some small snakes, but most won't even look at small mice. And force-feeding is impractical because their little bodies could never take the strain.

desert-dwellers, their ideal substrate is sand, although finely crushed walnut shells will also work well. Cage decor should include a few flat but light rocks (like shale) for the snakes to hide under, and a small waterbowl. They aren't great climbers, so plants and branches will only add visual beauty. A hidebox pretty much is unneccesary if you give a deep layer of substrate since these are burrowing animals. Heat is best provided via an undertank heating pad (a small

Hooknoses are rarely offered for sale, which is rather fortunate since they are a true challenge in captivity and really should be kept only by the most experienced hobbyists. In the above photo, you can see how the hooknose snakes got their name—the snout and upper jaw overlap ('hook over') the lower jaw. Both photos are of the Mexican Hooknose, *Ficimia strecker*.

one) or a spot lamp during the day, and a ceramic heat emitter can be used during the night, aimed at only one particular section of the enclosure. Temperature should be somewhere in the neighborhood of 85°F/30°C during the day, with a drop to about 77°F/25°C during the night. Photoperiod should be about ten to 12 hours of light per day.

scorpions. Since they are "bugivorous," let's say, it is impossible to wean them on to something easier to supply, like little mice for example. Every now and then, a specimen may turn up that will take small crickets, but I certainly wouldn't depend on this. The bottom line, like it or

As with the keeping of many other desert snakes, the main dilemma in keeping hooknoses is their diet—they are 'bugivores' that prefer generally unobtainable things like spiders and centipedes. They also have a fondness for scorpions, which *no* keeper should try to collect. Shown is a Desert Hooknose, *Gyalopion quadrangulare.*

Like longnose snakes, the major problem with keeping hooknoses lies in their feeding habits. In their case, it's not so much a question of their willingness to eat, but rather *what* they eat. According to both field and captive reports, hooknoses only eat centipedes, spiders, and

not, is that you will have to go out and actually collect either harmless spiders or centipedes (I'm not about to advise anyone to collect scorpions) if you want to keep a hooknose alive. If you live in an area where centipedes or harmless spiders are plentiful, then your problem is solved. If not, your problems are just beginning. The only good side to this is that, once given the items

Irritated hooknose specimens will twist and wiggle about when picked up, plus they have a talent for making popping sounds by everting their vent lining. Photos are of the Western Hooknose Snake, *Gyalopion canum.*

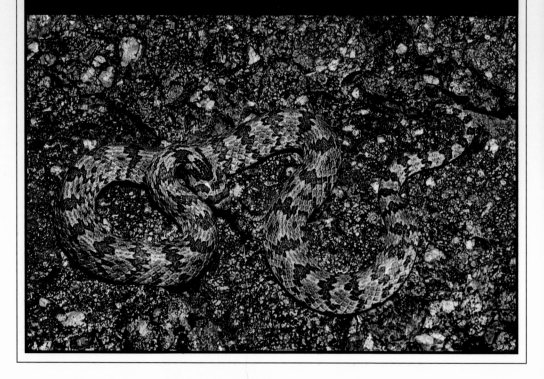

they want, hooknoses are voracious eaters.

Needless to say, captive breeding of the hooknoses has yet to be accomplished. In fact, very little is known about their reproductive cycle at all. They

Level 4—Hopelessly Impossible Stuff. Then I decided I didn't want to create any "doomsday" type of feelings towards any snake group. None are *impossible* to keep, some are just harder then others.

PHOTO BY R. D. BARTLETT.

Leafnose snakes, genus *Phyllorhynchus*, are relatively small (rarely over 20 in/50 cm), very attractive, and mild-tempered. So why are they so hard to maintain in captivity? Perhaps it's the fact that they eat only a few species of geckos and their eggs. Photo of a Spotted Leafnose Snake, *Phyllorhynchus decurtatus*.

apparently have very small egg clutches, and the young are impossibly tiny. If by chance you should come across a gravid specimen, it is urged that you incubate the eggs according to standard procedures, and carefully record all happenings. Such information would become valuable reference material to both keepers and scientists.

LEAFNOSE SNAKES
Genus *PHYLLORHYNCHUS* Stejneger, 1890
I considered putting these snakes in a "surprise" category—

However, the leafnoses probably are the toughest of all North American desert snakes. In fact, they probably are among the toughest of *any* snakes. Very few people have kept them with real success, and of those lucky few, none have ever bred them.

Their housing is the easy part. They grow only to about 20 in/ 50.8 cm, so a pair of adult specimens can be kept in a 20- or 30-gallon aquarium. Ideal substrates include sand, soil, or finely crushed walnut shells. Make sure the bedding is deep, because leafnoses are burrowers who will stress out if not giving the opportunity to dig down. Cage decor should include some flat, lightweight rocks (shale) and a few sturdy branches. A waterbowl also is necessary, plus a hidebox if you aren't going to offer the deep substrate. Heat can be provided via an undertank heating pad, and the temperature gradient should be from 80 to 85°F/26 to 30°C during the day, with about a four-degree drop during the night. Ten hours of light per day is the recommended photoperiod (and again, make sure the snakes have a very dark and secure place to hide during this time, because actual laboratory tests have shown that leafnoses are, for some odd reason, particularly sensitive to light, almost to the point where they seem terrified by it).

Okay, so now that the easy part has been illustrated, let's go right to the real nightmare—feeding. The problem with leafnoses in this respect is twofold. First, a leafnose's diet consists of some very weird items indeed. Second, even if you can supply those items, there's a very good chance they won't eat anyway. The items of wild specimens includes the tails and eggs of banded geckos, *Coleonyx* spp. Yes, that's right, the *tails* and *eggs* of banded geckos. Of course, many leafnose specimens will eat banded geckos whole, but others seem satisfied after grabbing one by the tail and having the tail snap off. Snakes that eat reptile eggs aren't *that* unusual, but they sure can cause a keeper plenty of angst when feeding time rolls around.

Some leafnoses can be trained to eat lizards other than geckos, but only after a long and tedious weaning period. Shown is a young Western Leafnose Snake, *Phyllorhynchus decurtatus perkinsi*, from the author's private collection. Photo by W. P. Mara.

Depending on the species you get, you may actually find one that will take geckos, and perhaps a select few other lizard species, but that's about as good as it's going to get with these guys. I have maintained two specimens for almost a year now on a beaten-chicken-egg diet, but I had to tube-feed them for the first four months, which I hate doing. Also, I have to include a rather generous portion of calcium supplementation to make up for the lack of same the snakes normally would get from lizards and their eggs. And again, even if you can somehow manage to supply a steady flow of lizards and lizard eggs, there still is the chance the snakes won't eat (like coral snakes, leafnoses seem to have a seething hatred for captivity).

Finally, breeding, as I said before, has never been achieved with these animals. That's kind of logical, actually—how can you breed them if you can't even keep them alive? There haven't even been that many gravid specimens found, so very little is known about their reproductive cycle. In early summer, they lay very small egg clutches—no more than five or six—and the young, which hatch in about 70 days, measure about 8 in/20 cm. It only can be assumed that the feeding habits of the newborns are similar to those of the adults.

A genuine and thoroughly documented captive history of any of the leafnose snakes, including a true captive breeding, would be a feather in any keeper's cap and a major breakthrough in modern herpetoculture.

THE REST OF THE GENERA

Included for the sake of completeness is a chart covering the remaining genera of North American colubrid snakes that contain desert-dwelling animals. Of course, the information given primarily refers to those particular snakes.

The Saddled Leafnose Snake, *Phyllorhynchus browni*, is virtually never seen in captivity and is as difficult to maintain as its generic brother, *P. decurtatus*. It is a nocturnal burrower that is most active (and most visible) in the spring. It shows itself mainly after heavy rains, during evening hours.

Anyone who has success with leafnose snakes should record all happenings and submit the data for publication. As with the keeping of many other desert snakes, reliable captive information on leafnoses is sparse at best. Any new information would be highly beneficial to both future hobbyists and the animals they keep.

	SIZE OR ENCLOSURE (FOR ONE ADULT PAIR)	RECOMMENDED SUBSTRATE	ENCLOSURE DECOR	DAY/NIGHT TEMPERATURE
BOGERTOPHIS Desert Rat Snakes Dowling & Price, 1988	30- or 55- gallon aquarium	Sand and gravel or soil and gravel	Branches, some rocks, a hidebox, and a waterbowl	80 to 85°F / 70 to 75°F
CROTALUS Rattlesnakes Linnaeus, 1758	55-gallon aquarium	Sand and gravel or only gravel	Large rocks, large hidebox, and a sturdy waterbowl	80 to 90°F / 72 to 78°F
SALVADORA Patchnose Snakes Baird & Girard, 1853	30- or 55- gallon aquarium	Sand or gravel	Branches, rocks, a hidebox, and a waterbowl	82 to 86°F / 74 to 78°F
CHILOMENISCUS Sand Snakes Cope, 1860	20- or 30- gallon aquarium	A deep layer of sand	A lot of flat rocks and a waterbowl	84 to 90°F / 70 to 75°F
HYPSIGLENA Night Snakes Cope, 1860	10- or 20- gallon aquarium	Sand and gravel or only sand	Rocks, a hidebox, a waterbowl, and one branch	82 to 86°F / 72 to 76°F
MASTICOPHIS Whipsnakes & Coachwhips Baird & Girard, 1853	55- gallon aquarium or outdoor enclosure	Sand, soil, or gravel	Branches, rocks, a waterbowl, and a large hidebox	80 to 85°F / 72 to 76°F
SONORA Ground Snakes Baird & Girard, 1853	10-gallon aquarium	Sand or soil	A lot of flat rocks and a waterbowl	78 to 84°F / 70 to 75°F
LEPTODEIRA Cat-eyed Snakes Fitzinger, 1843	20- or 30- gallon aquarium	Sand and gravel or soil	Branches, rocks, a waterbowl, and a large hidebox	84 to 90°F / 72 to 76°F
TANTILLA Blackhead & Crowned Snakes Baird & Girard, 1853	10-gallon aquarium	A deep layer of sand	A lot of flat rocks and a small waterbowl	82 to 86°F / 76 to 80°F

LEVEL 1 (BOGERTOPHIS, CROTALUS, SALVADORA)

LEVEL 2 (CHILOMENISCUS, HYPSIGLENA, MASTICOPHIS, SONORA)

LEVEL 3 (LEPTODEIRA, TANTILLA)

WILLING OR UNWILLING FEEDERS?	PREFERRED FOOD ITEMS	EGGLAYERS OR LIVE BEARERS?	TIME OF MATING	NUMBER OF EGGS OR YOUNG	MISCELLANEOUS NOTES
Willing	Lizards, birds, and rodents	Egglayers	Summer, with autumn egglaying	Two to eleven	Can be tempermental and nervous in captivity
Varies from species to species, but most are willing	Rodents	Livebearers	Usually spring or Summer	Three to twenty, but sometimes more	Obviously very dangerous; recommended only for professionals
Can be stubborn at first	Rodents, some reptiles	Egglayers	Spring	Four to ten	Most tame down and do very well
Willing	Small insects	Egglayers	Spring	Three to five	Surprisingly hardy captive that is rarely kept
Can be stubborn	Mostly small lizards, but some small frogs too	Egglayers	Usually spring, but sometimes late autumn	Four to six	Mildly venomous but harmless to humans. Hides during the day
Can be stubborn; many will only eat reptiles	Mostly reptiles, but sometimes rodents and birds as well	Egglayers	Spring	Four to eighteen	Very nasty and nervous
Willing, but food items may be tough to get	Insects, plus some insect pupae	Egglayers	Spring and autumn	Two to six	Once eating, they make good pets for youngsters
Willing, but food items may be tough to get	Mostly small frogs, but sometimes takes fish or mice	Egglayers	Early spring	Six to twelve	A true challenge even to the experienced keeper
Willing, but food items may be tough to get	Likes centipedes. Sometimes takes other small insects	Egglayers	Early spring	One to five	Strictly nocturnal and a very picky eater

Trans-Pecos Rat Snake, *Bogertophis subocularis*. Photo by K. H. Switak.

Trans-Pecos Rat Snake, *Bogertophis subocularis* ("blond" phase). Photo by R. D. Bartlett.

Western Diamondback Rattlesnake, *Crotalus atrox*. Photo by Zoltan Takacs.

Twin-spotted Rattlesnake, *Crotalus pricei pricei*. Photo by K. H. Switak.

Black-tailed Rattlesnake, *Crotalus molossus*. Photo by W. P. Mara.

Red Diamond Rattlesnake, *Crotalus ruber*. Photo by R. D. Bartlett.

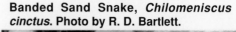

Banded Rock Rattlesnake, *Crotalus lepidus klauberi*. Photo by K. H. Switak.

Banded Sand Snake, *Chilomeniscus cinctus*. Photo by R. D. Bartlett.

Cerralvo Island Sand Snake, *Chilomeniscus savagei*. Photo by K. H. Switak.

Santa Catalina Night Snake, *Hypsiglena torquata catalinae*. Photo by K. H. Switak.

Texas Night Snake, *Hypsiglena torquata jani*. Photo by K. H. Switak.

Central Texas Whipsnake, *Masticophis taeniatus girardi*. Photo by R. D. Bartlett.

Western Coachwhip, *Masticophis flagellum testaceus*. Photo by Paul Freed.

Red Coachwhip, *Masticophis flagelleum piceus*. Photo by R. D. Bartlett.

Banded Cat-eyed Snake, *Leptodeira annulata*. Photo by R. D. Bartlett.

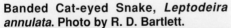

Flathead Snake, *Tantilla gracilis*. Photo by R. D. Bartlett

Plains Blackhead Snake, *Tantilla nigriceps*. Photo by W. P. Mara.

Coastal Dunes Crowned Snake, *Tantilla relicta pamlica*. Photo by R. D. Bartlett.

Ground Snake, *Sonora semiannulata*. Photo by W. P. Mara.

Ground Snake, *Sonora semiannulata* (ringed phase). Photo by John Iverson.

Ground Snake, *Sonora semiannulata* (ringed phase). Photo by R. D. Bartlett.

Night Snake, *Hypsiglena torquata*. Photo by W. P. Mara.

Mountain Patchnose Snake, *Salvadora grahamiae*. Photo by W. P. Mara.

Big Bend Patchnose Snake, *Salvadora deserticola*. Photo by R. D. Bartlett.

HOUSING CONSIDERATIONS

Since the focus of this book is on snakes that live in a specific environmental niche, it would be logical to begin the husbandry specifics with the topic of housing. The climate of desert snakes, generally speaking, can be described in one word—*dry*. Setting up and maintaining a dry terrarium really isn't all that difficult. Let's take a look at all aspects of setting up a desert terrarium, then you'll have a better grip on the subject as a whole.

SIZE OF THE ENCLOSURE

The snakes discussed in this book vary greatly in length, from the little ones such as the Mexican hooknose snakes, genus *Ficimia*, which grow to a length of around 11 in/28 cm, to the monsters of the genus *Pituophis*, which reach well over 6 ft/183 cm.

Knowing this, it is safe to say the size of the enclosure you invest in will depend largely on the snake(s) you're keeping. By following the simple chart offered here, you should get a fairly good idea of what size enclosure you should be looking for—

Length of Snake			Tank Size	
up	to	15 inches	10	gallon
16	to	25 inches	20	gallon
26	to	35 inches	30	gallon
36	to	55 inches	40	gallon
56	to	75 inches	55	gallon

Figuring the proper enclosure size is very important when housing snakes. Specimens that feel cramped will quickly become stressed and, as a result, probably will refuse food and eventually die. Photo of a Filetail Ground Snake, *Sonora aemula*.

PHOTO BY R. D. BARTLETT.

Larger snakes obviously need plenty of space in which to move around. If you place a large snake in tight confinement, chances are you will end up with very irritable animal that will not eat and soon die. If you do have a parcel of unused space that can be transformed into a viable holding pen, use it.

ENCLOSURE COMPONENTS

SUBSTRATES

What is the best substrate for desert snakes? Sand is the most logical choice. It can be purchased at any number of places (including pet shops), looks nice, and is great for absorbing moisture (i.e., moisture from feces). Also, any little section of sand that has been dirtied can be scooped out with a large spoon. Total replacement of a sand substrate need only be done once every few weeks. The downside to sand is that it is very heavy and thus difficult to deal with, especially when the intensive cleanings are required, but that's one of the prices you must pay to be a desert-terrarium enthusiast. Make sure the sand layer is deep since, as you already know, many desert-dwelling snakes need to burrow.

For the keeper who doesn't mind a slightly more "clinical" look and keeps those desert snakes that aren't burrowers, paper towels are an acceptable bedding. They are readily obtainable, absorbent, and easy

With many desert snakes, the simplest setup is the best setup. This pretty little Colorado Desert Shovelnose Snake, *Chionactis occipitalis annulata*, for example, needs only what is shown here—a deep sand layer, a small waterbowl, and a flat rock to hide under.

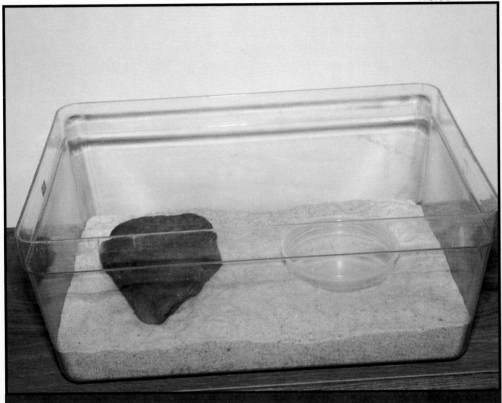

Most small desert snakes can be maintained in small enclosures, like this clear plastic sweaterbox. Such containers are inexpensive, easy to clean, and can be purchased in many places.

to work with. They are ideal for older keepers who may not have the strength the carry large glass aquariums filled with sand.

Along similar lines, it should be mentioned that many desert-dwelling snakes are quite small, and because of this they don't need to be kept in enormous enclosures. Thus, instead of an all-glass aquarium, a keeper can use a clear plastic sweaterbox. It can be filled with sand and still remain lightweight. A few small holes drilled through the lid or high on the sides (with either a drill or a soldering iron) will provide adequate ventilation.

Rocks

Rocks are necessary component for any snake's enclosure. Their essential purpose is to provide a snake with a rough surface on which to begin a shed. Unshed skin will cause infections, and, in a worse-case scenario, a snake that has not removed its eye caps might go blind.

Even in the most clinical-looking enclosures (paper towel substrate, plastic hidebox, and a waterbowl), there should be at least one rock. With naturalistic setups, there should be a few. With some desert-dwelling species, rocks are absolutely essential (as in the case of lyre snakes, genus *Trimorphodon*).

You can obtain rocks just about anywhere. Some pet shops carry choice examples that are particularly attractive. If your local shop doesn't have any, try a landscaper's supply house or a garden shop. If that proves fruitless, look around areas of undeveloped land (being careful, of course, to avoid private property).

Plants, Branches, Etc.

Plants and branches serve two purposes in snake enclosures. First, they make the arrangement seem more natural. But secondly, and perhaps more importantly, they provide objects to climb on. Obviously this latter point refers more to branches than plants since most plants available to the average keeper won't be able to

withstand the weight of a gopher snake or a fat old Coachwhip.

If you're aiming for a clinical setup over something more naturalistic, put in only a sturdy branch or two. If on the other hand your setup is a parcel of nature trapped in a glass box, then go for the full-blown horticultural project. Take the time to learn about what plants are found in the native environment of the snakes you're keeping. If you're diligent and creative, you'll end up with an enclosure so beautiful that you might not even notice the snakes anymore! This is a very easy situation to fall into because some desert landscapes are really quite impressive.

Waterbowls

Almost all snakes need a

Some desert-dwelling snakes are partially arboreal, like this Trans-Pecos Rat Snake, *Bogertophis subocularis* (represented here in a selectively bred "silver" form), and thus will need a few branches in their enclosure. Always do your homework on the daily habits of the snakes you keep. If you don't, you could run into problems. Arboreal snakes that aren't given anything to climb on, for example, probably will suffer severe stress.

PHOTO BY W. P. MARA.

PHOTO BY ZOLTAN TAKACS.

You can learn a great deal about how to properly house your desert snakes simply by studying their natural habitat. Go to the trouble of finding out exactly what kind of place they lived in, then try to replicate that environment in captivity. Photo of a desert habitat in Baja California.

waterbowl. The best are those with a wide base because they are hardest to tip. If you can't find one like this, try a heavy ceramic bowl. For larger snakes, you naturally should use a larger waterbowl.

One final note on this topic—since many desert setups need to be kept warm and dry, you may find yourself refilling waterbowls nearly every day because the water will evaporate so quickly. This should further illustrate how important good ventilation is because an enclosure with poor ventilation, a lot of heat, and a waterbowl will soon take on a pseudo-tropical air. And that, for many desert snakes, will spell death.

Hideboxes

The purpose of a hidebox, obviously, is to provide a snake with a place in which to hide. Many desert-dwelling snakes don't even need a hidebox in the first place simply because they burrow into their substrate when they want privacy.

Other species, however, definitely need a hiding place. General guidelines to follow include making sure very little light gets inside the hidebox. Also, a keeper should avoid going into the box when the animal's in there. You can make hideboxes from plastic shoe or sweaterboxes, or you can make use of more naturalistic materials like a group of rocks cemented together. Don't just pile a bunch of rocks on top

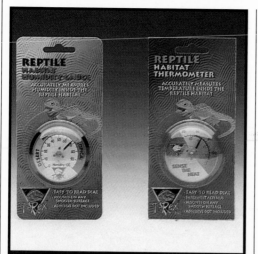

Keeping an eye on the ambient temperature and humidity of a snake's enclosure is an important facet of good husbandry. Fortunately, high-range thermometers and hygrometers designed specifically for herp-keeping are now available. Photo courtesy of Ocean Nutrition.

of each other until you've got a cave. It only takes a little pressure to send such a structure tumbling down, possibly on the unfortunate specimen that happens to be inside at the time.

CLIMATE CONTROL

Heating

All desert snakes need heat. During the warmer parts of the year, you may be able to provide it simply by opening the window in your snake room. In colder months, however, you will have to provide heat artificially. The ideal temperature for the snakes discussed in this book varies tremendously. Generally speaking, however, most North American desert-dwelling snakes

The desert can be a sweltering place during the day and a chilly place during the night. Thus, it is important that you provide some sort of 'cooling period' on a nightly basis. Many desert snakes are nocturnal specifically because they cannot handle the heat of the day. Photo of Joshua Tree National Park.

PHOTO BY ZOLTAN TAKACS.

will remain happy and healthy with a daytime temperature of between 85 and 95°F/28 and 35°C. It also should be pointed out that there needs to be a slight drop in temperature during the night. The nighttime gradient should be around 78 to 84°F/25 to 29°C.

There are many products designed to help you warm a snake's enclosure. The best, in my opinion anyway, is the undertank heating pad. The main advantage to using one is that only a certain area of the enclosure will be heated, which affords a snake the freedom to move onto or away from it at will. Another nice point is the fact that undertank heating pads can be used without any

dissension to tank security (e.g., in the case of "heated rocks," running an electrical cord into the enclosure, thus creating a gap between the enclosure's rim and the lid).

I'll give you a helpful hint concerning heating pads—there are some that are designed to stick to the bottom of a glass tank, but the adherent substance is *so* adherent, you'll never be able to get the pad off again! So here's a solution—wrap the pad in tin foil. Then all you have to do is slip it under the tank when you want to use it, and slip it back out when you're done.

Another heating item is a *spot lamp*, which, aimed at a certain area, creates a basking spot. Heat

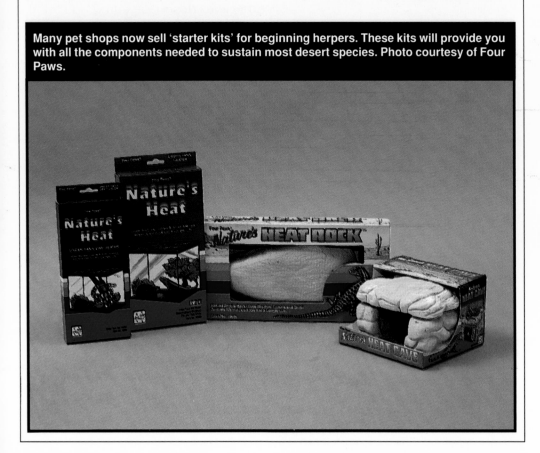

Many pet shops now sell 'starter kits' for beginning herpers. These kits will provide you with all the components needed to sustain most desert species. Photo courtesy of Four Paws.

lamps are offered at many pet shops and usually are reasonably priced. They are very useful in the keeping of many herptiles (especially lizards). You can replicate the natural effect of the sun by setting up a spot lamp along with a timer.

Finally, ambient heat, provided by a small "space heater," will satisfy the needs of many desert-dwelling snakes. Ceramic heaters are the best for this purpose. They are small, inexpensive, and cost-effective as far as your electric bill is concerned. Make sure the heater is connected to a thermostat (some have thermostats already built in) so your snake room doesn't get *too* hot.

Lighting (Photoperiod)

By loose definition, photoperiod means "the amount of daylight an animal is exposed to." The snakes discussed in this book should get about ten to 12 hours of light per day, less towards autumn if you plan to breed them.

The easiest way to make sure your snakes get the correct photoperiod is by hooking up your lighting apparatus to a timer. This will relieve you of the responsibility of turning the lights on and off. Timers can be purchased at most any department store, hardware store, or home-improvement center.

Desert snakes that are active during the daytime should be given some form of heat that radiates from above their heads so as to replicate the way they get their heat in the wild. Shown is Big Bend National Park in western Texas.

PHOTO BY K. H. SWITAK.

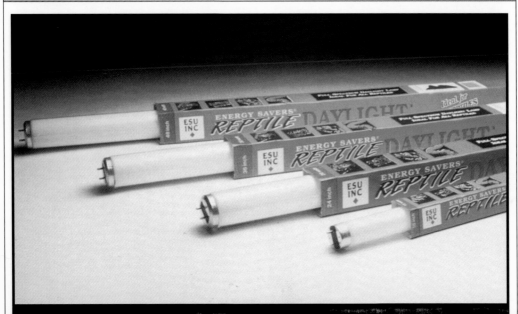

Providing your desert snakes with the correct photoperiod (day/night cycle) is very important. Photoperiod is often a factor in determining a herptile's behaviorisms. Bulbs designed specifically for the keeping of reptiles and amphibians now are available at many pet shops. Photo courtesy of Energy Savers.

Quality of light needn't be anything more than ordinary tungsten. If you've ever kept turtles or lizards, then you know what "full-spectrum" lighting is— light that replicates that given off by the sun. What this light does is aid a turtle or a lizard in the production of vitamin D3, which they need in order to survive.

But snakes don't need such light. It is worth mentioning, however, that a few professional breeders claim that snakes exposed to full-spectrum lighting for about five or six hours per day have better breeding results. The improvement seems to be in the snakes' willingness to breed, the hardiness of the eggs, and the size of the clutch. What it all comes down to in the end is that a little full-spectrum lighting won't really harm your snakes either way.

Don't forget, however, that nocturnal snakes obviously won't benefit very much from full-spectrum lighting because they'll be hiding when it's shining, so they won't benefit very much from it either way.

ENCLOSURE MAINTENANCE

The enclosure of a desert snake (or any other captive animal, for that matter) must be frequently cleaned; *at least* once a week is recommended. A filthy enclosure will promote all sorts of health problems.

Here's a simple, step-by-step method of cleaning a snake's enclosure that I've used it for many years. The results always have been satisfying.

1) Take the occupants out of the enclosure and place them in a secure holding area. Try a deep

If you are looking for a substrate that is easy to work with a terrarium liner will do nicely. Many pet shops now carry these, and in different sizes so as to fit different-sized enclosures. They work well with desert species who do not burrow. Photo courtesy of Four Paws.

plastic bucket or garbage can with a tight-fitting lid.

2) Remove all climate-control equipment. This includes heating devices, lights, and so on. Since these items use electricity, they should be kept well away from the tank, which soon will be filled with water.

3) Remove all other components. Disposing of the disposables, and placing the reusables in a bucket.

4) Cleanse the empty tank thoroughly using a mixture of warm water, dish soap, and a splash of household bleach. The bleach takes care of all the really nasty germs, while the soap does more of the superficial cleaning. Use a sponge or an old rag, but not a scrub pad for it will scratch the glass. If you have any stubbornly adherent matter, let it soak in the water/soap/bleach mixture for a few minutes. If that doesn't help, carefully chip it off the big pieces a plastic knife, then moisten the remaining filthy spot until it softens.

5) Rinse the tank in cold water, and rinse it well. The last thing a snake needs is bleach residue on its skin. Also be sure the tank is *completely dry.*

6) Now clean the reusable items (except those made of wood) using the same procedure outlined in steps four and five. Wood items can be cleaned by scraping away large pieces of fecal matter and then sanding the remaining spot with a sheet of medium-grade sandpaper.

7) Set up the enclosure again.

8) Now you either can place the snakes back into their enclosure, or you can bathe them and *then* stick them back in their enclosure. Does the idea of bathing a snake sound strange? It shouldn't. Consider the fact that snakes get fecal matter on themselves just as easily as they do on everything else. Also consider that skin infections can develop. Bathing a snake gives its keeper the chance to inspect it, looking for early signs of illness, abrasions, cuts, scars, skinniness, and things like that. I like to think of it as a weekly health inspection.

A sensible bathing procedure doesn't involve any kind of soaps, powders, or perfumes. All you really need to do is fill up a little tub with some warm water, slosh the snakes around in it for a few minutes, then dry them with a soft towel. The whole process doesn't take much time and only encourages a snake's health.

PHOTO BY ISABELLE FRANCAIS.

All snake tanks need to be cleaned regularly; unsanitary enclosures quickly become a breeding ground for health problems. Give your snakes' tanks a good washing every two weeks at least.

Snakes whose bodies are kept clean (i.e., are given occasional baths) rarely fall prey to any external problems like fungal development or dysecdysis. Also, a keeper who bathes his or her snakes gets the chance to run regular inspections of their specimens. Photo of a Spotted Leafnose Snake, *Phyllorhynchus decurtatus*.

PHOTO BY K. H. SWITAK.

FEEDING

Perhaps the greatest hurdle to be overcome in the keeping of desert snakes is feeding. While some desert-snake species are ravenous feeders of easy-to-supply items like mice and crickets, others have highly specialized diets that will drive keepers out of their minds.

However, many techniques have been developed to aid the unfortunate soul who has gotten stuck with a stubborn or highly specialized feeder. Again, it is my opinion that feeding is the most difficult aspect of keeping the snakes of the North American deserts, but once a specimen (or specimens) is on a regular diet, everything will be a breeze from that point on.

THE FOOD ITEMS

Mice and Rats

Mice and rats are sort of the "standard" food of captive snakes. Both offer high nutrition and can be obtained in bulk quantities, and of varying size, at most pet shops.

There is a somewhat controversial question concerning them—are they best offered alive or dead? If you have obtained a large quantity of them frozen, then there isn't much of a decision to be made, is there? But what about when you've acquired them live? Should they then be killed before being offered?

Most keepers say yes. By doing this, you eliminate the possibility of the mouse or rat harming the

Frozen rodents, which can be thawed a few different ways, not only are nutritious for snakes, they also are convenient for the keeper. They can be purchased in neat packages and kept in the freezer. And, most snakes that take rodents live can be trained to accept them thawed as well. Photo courtesy of Ocean Nutrition.

snake. On the other hand, however, other keepers like to make a snake work for its food, particularly since snakes tend to become lethargic in captivity and build up a lot of fat.

Nevertheless, frozen-and-thawed rodents seem to be the more popular with hobbyists. Defrosting them is easy—soak them in a bowl of hot tap water. Complete defrostation occurs usually takes no more than thirty minutes. remove the rodent from the water, dry it with a towel, and serve. Some keepers claim they defrost their frozen rats and mice in a microwave, but those of us who still adhere to some standards of good taste opt for the saner hot-water technique.

One final issue—if you decide you want to offer your snakes only pre-killed rodents yet have access only to live ones and don't like the idea of killing them, try this—place a set mouse or rat trap in a bucket (making sure the baited end of the trap is against the bucket wall), drop in the rodent in question, put the lid back on, and wait for the inevitable.

Lizards

Many desert snakes eat lizards, which is quite logical if you consider how many lizards are slithering around the deserts of North America. The problem, of course, is how to supply lizards on a regular basis. If you live in an area where lizards are common, you can trap them simply by sinking a large plastic garbage can into the ground,

Adding a little powdered calcium supplement to your desert snakes' food items every now and then isn't a bad idea. You either can sprinkle the powder right onto the food items or include it in the food items' diet. Photo courtesy of American Reptile.

making sure the rim is level with the ground and there are a few holes drilled through the bottom for water drainage.

However, if you don't live in an area where lizards are common, what can you do? Well, you could go to a pet shop and buy them. Of course, unless your local pet shop offers "feeder lizards" at a special discount price (which I strongly doubt), you'll probably be filing for bankruptcy within a few weeks. Another approach is to contact your local herp society and see if anyone there can lead you in the direction of some low-priced lizards.

But the best method, at least in my experience, is simply to "scent" a more easily obtainable food item (like a frozen-and-

PHOTO BY W. P. MARA.

Lizards are a common dietary element of many desert snakes. Of course, most keepers will not be able to supply lizards on a regular basis. If you can, however, you should do so; they are very nutritious. Photo of a *Rhinocheilus lecontei "clarus"* devouring a *Sceloporus undulatus*.

thawed mouse) by rubbing it on the body of a live (or, again, frozen-and-thawed) lizard until that item has taken on the lizard smell. Along very similar lines, some keepers claim scenting success by maintaining a colony of lizards and smearing the other food items in the lizards' feces. Either way, scenting is a fairly reliable technique that can conceivably enable you to successfully maintain many snakes that otherwise would be out of the question.

"Bugs"

Bugs, which is what I will call creepy-crawly creatures like spiders, centipedes, millipedes, ants, and the like, are a surprisingly common dietary component of many desert-dwelling snakes. In fact, I'd go so far as to say anyone interested in maintaining snakes in a desert terrarium must be prepared to supply a variety of "bugs" or else your success will be dishearteningly limited.

Let's start with the standard— the cricket. A cricket offers a snake a highly nutritious meal. Crickets can be purchased in quantity (and usually in various sizes) at virtually any pet shop that carries herptiles. There are quite a few desert-dwelling snake species that accept crickets on a regular basis, and some will even take them frozen-and-thawed! If you are fortunate enough to acquire such a snake, it is advised that you purchase crickets in bulk quantity and freeze them right away. That way, if you buy 500 crickets, you'll get to use 500 crickets. If you buy 500 and maintain them alive, in under a month at least half will die in their enclosure and quickly be consumed by the others. An easy way to defrost frozen crickets is to lay them on a heating pad for about fifteen minutes.

Mealworms and waxworms are eaten by a few desert snakes. Like the aforementioned cricket, they can be purchased in large quantities at many pet shops. Mealworms can be cultured in the home without too much trouble.

Housing should consist of a plastic shoebox or sweaterbox half-filled with some sort of grain or bran material (oatmeal always worked well for me). For increased nutritional purposes, also add in a few slices of apple or orange, these being thrown out and replaced every five or six days. Begin the colony with about two-hundred adult mealworms (which often are called "king" mealworms). These will pupate into the hard-shelled adults and begin breeding at once. As your initial colony begins to grow, skim off the excess worms and use them to start new colonies. In a relatively short time, you'll have so many mealworms you won't

Sometimes desert snakes become the eaten rather than the eaters. Here, a ground snake, *Sonora*, is being fed upon by a centipede. This illustrates one good reason why you should train your snakes to accept food pre-killed rather than live—you never know when the food item is going to be hungrier (and more dangerous) than the snake!

PHOTO BY WILLIAM B. ALLEN, JR.

know what to do with them all!

Realistically, spiders, ants (and their pupae), centipedes, millipedes, and a variety of other such critters, can only be obtained in the field (by turning over boards and stones, breaking up rotted logs, digging through leaf litter and chip piles, etc.). Perhaps there is a lone culturist somewhere who actually maintains and even breeds such animals, but for the average keeper, the only person within reach who offers a regular supply is Mother Nature.

It should be pointed out that anyone going into the field to collect livefoods should learn to recognize all dangers that might be waiting them. In other words, make sure whatever livefoods you collect can't harm you (e.g., the Black Widow spider, which has caused human death on many occasions). Specimens are best held in a glass or plastic container with tiny holes drilled through the lid for ventilation. Most creatures of this ilk are quite nutritious. The only problem you may have is supplying them on a regular basis. Some of the tinier

desert snakes need to eat every few days, and stories about not being able to find any food for them won't fill their stomachs.

Vitamin Supplements

A little bit of vitamin powder or liquid should be included in the diet of *any* captive snake. Many snakes simply will not get all their

required nutrients from their food items, so you must give them vitamin supplements in order to keep them healthy. Vitamin supplements should be included about once every three or four meals. Only use a little each time—a

PHOTO BY K. H. SWITAK.

Desert snakes should be fed every three to five days (young specimens a little more frequently than adults). If a particular specimen displays glutinous tendencies, however, don't indulge it. Obesity can very easily cause death in captive reptiles. Photo of a Night Snake, *Hypsiglena torquata*, eating a Fence Swift, *Sceloporus undulatus.*

few drops of liquid or just a pinch of powder. Overdoing it can have drastic consequences, sometimes leading an animal to an early death.

Some keepers wonder 'Which form of vitamins is superior, powder or liquid?' There's no definite answer here. It really depends on the needs of each person. I prefer the powder only because it's easier to use—I moisten a pre-killed food item, then sprinkle on the powder. Also, when I freeze large quantities of crickets for my shovelnose snakes, I put a heaping teaspoonful of both multivitamin and calcium powder in the container and shake it all around beforehand. But again, if you find the liquid vitamins are better for your particular situation, then by all means use them. Both forms can be purchased at pet shops that carry herpetocultural goods.

HOW MUCH, HOW OFTEN?

The question of how much a snake needs to eat and how often is a common one. Do larger snakes get fed more often, or do they just get more food per feeding? What about very small snakes? Do they need less food because they're so small, or more because they generally have a 'faster' metabolism?

The answer to all these questions can be found only in the keeper's instinct. You will have to experiment with each snake to develop a 'feel' for how much he or she eats and how often. Some snakes literally are food-disposal units, gorging themselves until even the simplest movements become laborious. Others seem to know what their limit is and will eat only enough to fill their needs at that moment. Obviously, the more piggish snakes should not be overfed or else they'll become obese and eventually die. On the other hand, a snake that eats 'just enough' can be a cause of great stress to its keeper. It will never become satisfyingly

PHOTO BY W. P. MARA.

Maintaining and culturing your own mealworms is fairly easy. You need a large plastic container, some grain or oat material (here, ordinary store-brand oatmeal was used), and a few slices of fruit. Keep a lid on the container with a few holes drilled through it.

plump and will grow very, very slowly.

As a rule, I try to feed all my snakes every four days. I offer enough so they can eat as much as they want, then stop when they want. I guess what I'm shooting for with this approach is to take the whole problem off my shoulders and let them figure it out. I've already identified the 'piggy' specimens and feed them separately. The others, however, I can trust to eat enough, but not too much.

CAPTIVE BREEDING

As I said in the introduction, many of the snakes found in the deserts of North America have never been bred in captivity, so maybe you will want to give one or two of them a try. If someone was to try writing a book on the complete captive-breeding history of every snake in the world, there would be so many gaps in the text it would be pathetic. There are thousands and thousands of snake species, yet so few are ever domestically cultured. Hopefully this will change in coming years.

CHOOSING BREEDER SPECIMENS

Only the highest-quality specimens should be considered for a breeding program. If you've read through the rest of the text then you know what it takes to culture high-quality specimens—a varied diet, a proper climate, regular health checks, attentiveness to cleanliness, and so on. Unhealthy snakes not only can't produce viable eggs or sperm, they probably won't even survive hibernation, which is brutally stressful on even the healthiest specimens. Other obvious points include the fact that breeder snakes need to be well-accustomed to captive life, sexually mature, of adult size, and of compatible size.

HIBERNATION

Virtually all North American snakes must go through a period of hibernation before they breed. If they don't, they will be unable to produce viable sperm (males) and fertile eggs (females). The hibernation process acts as a recharging period. Without it, a pair of snakes may still mate, but no eggs, or at best a clutch of infertile eggs, will be produced.

First you must prepare the 'hibernaculum,' i.e., the place where the snakes will hibernate. This can be anything from the glass tank the snakes usually stay in to a custom-built wooden crate. I've always used plastic sweaterboxes with a few holes drilled through the lid. Beddings vary with other colubrids, but again, since we're dealing with desert snakes here, sand is the best (or, if for some reason you feel the need to use something else, soil). Other components include a hidebox and a small bowl of water, which the snakes will in fact drink from, believe it or not.

Now the snakes themselves must be properly prepared. Most importantly, they must be completely devoid of any fecal material. Stop feeding them about two weeks before the hibernation process is scheduled to begin. Then, during the last week, bathe them for about an hour each day in warm water. This will loosen up and flush out any remaining waste matter. This step is important because waste matter remaining in a system that has been slowed down by the hibernation process will ferment, infect the intestinal walls, and kill the host.

Now actual hibernation begins. Drop the snakes' ambient temperature *slowly*, e.g., about five degrees each day. The temperature you're shooting for with most North American desert-dwelling species is somewhere between 50 and 55°F/10 and 13°C. The hibernaculum should be kept in relative darkness and relative quiet. Cellars and attics are good places for this. Don't disturb the 'sleepers' except to change their water and check up on their health. Needless to say, if a snake begins to rapidly lose weight during the hibernation term, remove it, warm it up, and begin feeding it again.

Hibernation should last around two months. Any less than seven weeks is risky, and any more than ten weeks probably is unnecessary (and sometimes dangerous, especially with small specimens). When the hibernation period is over, bring the snakes back up to their active-season temperature the same slowly progressive way you eased them into it. Allow them a day or two to reorient themselves (and perhaps shed), then begin offering food as usual.

MATING

Shortly after the term of hibernation has been completed, mating can begin. Even for snakes that have never been bred before, you can pretty much assume the procedure is 'standard' as for most North American colubrids.

It is best to place a female into a male's enclosure rather than the reverse. Sometimes females can be quite territorial, and those that occasionally include reptiles in their diet just might eat their 'mates!' Ideally, however, the male should begin rubbing himself against the female in a jerky, spasmodic fashion. Then he may crawl along her back while twisting his tail around hers in an attempt to align their cloacas so he can insert one of his hemipenes. The female may not allow penetration at first, but after a time she should calm down and submit. If after about an hour no mating takes place, remove the female and try the pair again the next day. Once started, copulation can last from fifteen minutes to a full hour. In extreme cases, it can reach up to two or three hours. It should also be noted that many desert snakes only breed under the cover of darkness, so you may want to introduce a female to a male during the night hours.

Some keepers wonder, 'Is it okay for me to stay and watch the mating?' The answer is yes, mainly for safety reasons. Sometimes snakes fight, especially when a female is not in the mood to breed but the male keeps 'pushing' her. Also, there are times when, after the snakes are finished, they have trouble separating. In such cases you may have to immerse them in a shallow pan of warm water, which will help relax the swollen, uh...'parts.'

Watching snakes breed will be fascinating for any herpetoculturist, but it should be done from a reasonable distance.

Snakes caught up in the 'breeding trance' probably won't even notice you, but why take that chance? Unless something seems to be going wrong, stay at least five to ten feet from the enclosure. And remember, since many desert snakes only breed during the night, you might not get the chance to see them anyway. In such a case, your only alternative is to place a dim red light above the enclosure and hope the snakes aren't distracted by it. Many snakes seem to have a problem recognizing red light, a fact revealed through breeding experiments conducted by zoos.

THE GRAVID FEMALE

The first rule for dealing with gravid snakes is *don't handle them unless you absolutely have to.* By ignoring this rule you risk premature laying of bad eggs or deformed young. Patience is a virtue during here.

A female should have her own quarters—private, dark, and a little warmer than normal. She'll need that extra heat for her developing embryos. Offer food to her as you would during any other time of the year, but keep in mind that some pregnant females may refuse food. However, as long your specimen is not losing weight, don't let her lack of appetite bother you. If she is losing weight, bring her to a vet.

EGGLAYING AND LIVE BIRTHS

During the final weeks of the gestation period for oviparous snakes (i.e., snakes that lay eggs rather than give birth to live young, the latter being known as *viviparous* snakes), the mother will need something called an egglaying box. This can be as simple as a plastic shoe or sweaterbox with a bedding of moistened vermiculite or sphagnum moss, or a combination of both (or, indeed, moistened sand). Place the box in the female's enclosure and give her time to become comfortable with it. In the case of burrowing desert species, you should keep the box's lid on with an entrance hole cut through it. Most desert species lay their eggs in subterranean chambers, and this setup will replicate that sensation of 'going underground.' (Actually, you could conceivably take this a step further and bury the eggbox in the substrate so only the entrance hole is exposed.)

Keep in mind that if you don't provide an egglaying box, the mother just might lay her eggs in some dry corner of her enclosure (which wouldn't be too hard to find in a desert terrarium), where they will quickly spoil. Also, be sure you remove the eggbox so none of the mothers decide to make a meal out of what's inside (which happens more often than you might imagine).

In the case of viviparous species, there's really not a lot you can do to prepare the mother other than give her the aforementioned increased privacy and warmth. No special 'laying box' will be needed. Most live-bearing snakes kept in captivity give birth during the night, in the security of darkness. This is rather unfortunate since the sight of a snake being born is absolutely fascinating. Keep in mind that since many desert snakes are rather small, their offspring will be nearly microscopic, so it is best that you separate the latter from their 'birthing' enclosure and set them up in their own as soon as possible. Like the eggs, they just might end up becoming a meal for the adults.

EGG INCUBATION

As long as you've used the proper substrate, an egglaying box can double as an incubation box. As a rule, you should always be sure the substrate is moist (not wet, just moist), and, whatever else you do, *don't* turn the eggs. They must remain in the exact position in which they were laid. If you can, separate the eggs before they adhere in a cluster. That way, if one goes bad, you can throw it out before it has the chance to infect the others.

Also important is adequate ventilation. A few small holes drilled through the lid will suffice. Check the substrate every other day to make sure it's still moist. If it begins to dry (which it periodically will), hydrate it with a spray bottle filled with warm water, remembering not to mist the eggs themselves.

Ideal incubation temperature is around 75°F/24°C. Length of incubation varies from genus to genus (sometimes species to species), so you'll have to do a little research concerning the snake you have. Average for North

Most desert snakes will lay their eggs under the cover of darkness. So, when you have a female that you know to be gravid, give her an added measure of privacy. Stressed snakes may lay their eggs prematurely, and the eggs probably will be spoiled as a result. Photo of a Spotted Night Snake, *Hypsiglena torquata ochrorhynchus*

PHOTO BY J. K. LANGHAMMER.

American colubrids is somewhere around 75 days, but again, that has the potential to vary tremendously. Immediately after the eggs hatch, you'll see the neonates crawling around near their shells with their umbilical cord still attached. Within a day or so the cord will dry up and break off. It is after this time that you then may take the snakes out of the eggbox and place them in their new (and separate from the adults) enclosure.

CARE OF THE YOUNG

The final hurdle in the breeding of desert snakes is to get the newborns feeding on their own. With most other snakes this is fairly easy, but since many desert-dwelling species have highly specialized diets, the whole matter becomes a bit more complicated.

Fortunately, many neonatal desert snakes eat the same things their parents do, so if you've already got adult specimens, then all you really need to do is offer scaled-down versions of whatever they've been getting. For example, neonatal shovelnose snakes, *Chionactis* spp., will accept very tiny crickets (pinheads), just as the adults will

PHOTO BY ISABELLE FRANCAIS.

If and when you manage to get a pair of snakes mating, leave them alone while they're together. Many snakes do not appreciate being observed during this time and will not respond to each other because they're too busy watching you.

accept those that are full-grown. Similarly, neonatal Gray-banded Kingsnakes, *Lampropeltis alterna*, will gladly accept tiny lizards, keeping in step with the 'lizardivorous' nature of their parents.

If you end up with a neonate that won't take the same foods the adults have been accepting, don't become alarmed. Stop and puzzle the problem out logically. Remember that snakes in the wild almost always have a fairly varied diet, meaning a snake that eats only mice in captivity may eat a lot more than that in nature. For example, if you've trained your hooknose snake to eat only crickets, don't be surprised when its offspring refuses them. Check a reliable reference guide to see what else that particular snake eats when its wild and free. That probably is where your answer lies. Remember—the priority is to get the newborns eating at any cost. You can worry about weaning them onto other things later.